THE LEMONADE STAND

by Claire Daniel

illustrated by Len Epstein

SCHOOL PUBLISHERS

Printed in China

ISBN 10: 0-15-350317-3
ISBN 13: 978-0-15-350317-7

Ordering Options
ISBN 10: 0-15-349941-9 (Grade 6 ELL Collection)
ISBN 13: 978-0-15-349941-8 (Grade 6 ELL Collection)
ISBN 10: 0-15-357361-9 (package of 5)
ISBN 13: 978-0-15-357361-3 (package of 5)

5 6 7 8 9 10   0940   12 11 10 09

Jeff and Oscar flipped through the large stack of comic books in Jeff's room. One by one, they tossed each comic book aside.

"Let's go to the store and buy some more comic books," Jeff told his friend Oscar. "I've read all these comics so many times that I've memorized them!"

"I'm tired of my comic book collection, too," said Oscar. "I don't have any money to buy more comic books, though."

Jeff checked his pockets and found only a quarter. "I don't have much money either," he said sadly.

"I have an idea," Jeff said. "Let's set up a stand outside the house. We can sell these old comic books. Then we can use the money from the sales to buy new ones."

Jeff and Oscar took their old comic books outside and placed them on a table. Then the boys hung up a large sign that said, "Comic Books For Sale."

Jeff's house was the last house on the block. Few cars came by all day. Only one boy looked at the comic books. He said that he already had them all, so he didn't buy anything.

The boys' friend Zareen walked by after a while. She flipped through the comic books. "How is business?" she asked.

"It's terrible!" Oscar said. "One person came by. However, he wasn't interested in anything."

"Can I make a suggestion?" Zareen asked.

"Yes, please," Jeff said. "We haven't sold anything all day!"

"You need to be in a place where people can see you. Not many people pass by this place," Zareen said. "Why don't we move to my front walk? It's in the center of town. A lot more people pass through my neighborhood. It's a good location." Oscar and Jeff agreed.

5

"I have another idea," Zareen said. "I'll make pitchers of lemonade, too. Then we will have more than one thing to sell! People might stop for the lemonade if they are thirsty. Then they will look at your comic books."

"That's a terrific idea!" Oscar said.

"Also, you need to remove any damaged copies in your collection," Zareen said. "People will not want to buy your comic books if they think they are all damaged."

Zareen's ideas were good ones. Oscar and Jeff moved the comic book table to her front walk and put up a huge sign to advertise the sale.

Many people went by Zareen's apartment. Soon people began to stop to buy lemonade from Oscar, Jeff, and Zareen. Joggers passed by and were thirsty. Bikers stopped because they were hot and tired. Some people from the hot dog stand across the street saw the new stand. Even they came over to buy lemonade.

Business started out well on the second day, too. Then Henry, the owner of the hot dog stand, came over from across the street. He looked angry.

"I want you to move out of here!" he said. "You are taking away my customers! No one is buying drinks at my hot dog stand. They buy a hot dog. Then they cross the street to your stand to buy your lemonade."

"Maybe your drinks are too expensive," Oscar suggested.

"No, I think that my customers want to help you because you are kids," Henry said. "Also, they see your sign before they reach my hot dog stand. I have to earn money to take care of my family. You are taking away my sales!"

"Henry, I think we can work together," said Zareen. "What if we put up a sign to advertise your hot dog stand? We could publicize your business along with ours. People who weren't going to buy a hot dog may come and buy one."

"I'm not sure that will work," Henry said.

"Okay, I have another idea," Zareen said. "We can raise the price of our lemonade by twenty cents. Then we will give you the extra money that we make."

"I would get twenty cents for every cup of lemonade that you sell?" Henry asked. "Why?"

"We don't want you to lose money because of us," Zareen said. "We are also grateful that your business helps our business."

"Also, if you give us a sample hot dog then we'll advertise how good your hot dogs are," Oscar said.

Henry thought for a minute. "You've got a deal," he said.

Henry brought over three hot dogs covered with chili, relish, mustard, and ketchup. Zareen gave Henry a glass of lemonade to drink while she and the boys ate their hot dogs.

"Delicious!" Oscar and Jeff said together.

"These hot dogs are juicy and tasty," Zareen said enthusiastically. "I will have an easy time telling people that these hot dogs are good!"

Oscar and Jeff went to work right away. They made a huge sign that read, "Enjoy a delicious hot dog from Henry's with your lemonade!" Zareen drew a picture of a huge hot dog and a glass of lemonade on the banner.

As the summer continued, more and more people stopped by the kids' lemonade stand. Jeff, Oscar, and Zareen often ran out of supplies to make lemonade. One of the three kids always needed to go to the store to buy more lemons, ice, sugar, and water. Jeff, Oscar, and Zareen began to realize that to make money they needed to spend money on these important supplies. The lemonade stand taught the three a lot about starting a business. Now they felt ready to try something new.

One day a girl's bicycle tire became flat right in front of the lemonade stand. Oscar offered to help the girl fix her bicycle. Then he looked at the rest of the bike. "You also need to oil your chain, or you will have trouble with your bike," he said.

Jeff and Oscar looked at each other. They both had the same idea at the very same moment! They wouldn't spend their profits from the stand on new comic books. They would use the money to start a bicycle repair stand instead!

The next day, Jeff and Oscar set up their bicycle repair stand next to Zareen's lemonade stand. Many bikers used the bike paths in the park nearby. Some of the bikers needed bike repairs from time to time.

The summer passed quickly. The children had made quite a lot of money by the end of August.

"Thanks, Zareen," Oscar said. "We made this money because of your advice."

"I need to thank you," Zareen said. "You had the idea to start a business!"

Scaffolded Language Development

QUOTATION MARKS Review with students the punctuation in these sentences from the story:

"Let's go to the store and buy some more comic books," Jeff told his friend Oscar. (page 3)

"Can I make a suggestion?" Zareen asked. (page 5)

"That's a terrific idea!" Oscar said. (page 6)

Remind students that quotation marks show exactly what a speaker says. Question marks, commas, and exclamation points go inside the end quote.

Have students rewrite these sentences with quotation marks in the appropriate places.

1. I want to get some new comic books, Oscar said to Jeff.
2. What are you doing here? Henry wanted to know.
3. Scram! Get lost! Henry yelled.
4. Zareen asked, What's wrong?
5. Jeff, Oscar, and Zareen cheered, Hooray! Our new business is a success!

Have students chorally read the sentences aloud.

⭐ Language Arts

Work Together! Have students make a list of three positive characteristics of the children in the story. Then have students write a letter to the editor of a newspaper telling the community about the kids and what they did.

School-Home Connection

For Sale Have students discuss cooperation with a friend or family member. Encourage them to discuss the project in the story and how it turned out.

Word Count: 1,093